MINDSET TO WEALTH

GET WEALTHY FOR SURE

MICHAEL LINDELL

A New Mindset to Wealth:

Get Wealthy for Sure

ISBN 9798569766925

You may order additional copies for you and your team by emailing service@themichaellindell.com

First Edition

CONTENTS

Preface

My vision is to teach people how to increase their income by altering their mind. I've spent the last few years of my life giving strategies on how to overcome mindset adversities that individuals need to succeed in life, particularly, in their finances.

The purpose of this booklet, *A New Mindset to Wealth*, is to provide individuals with effective tools to gain greater satisfaction and knowledge that will help them move to extraordinary financial levels.

I hope this booklet will help you achieve your financial goals.

This booklet highlights the importance of having the right mindset. It shows how the right set of thoughts can improve mental health and increase the chances of financial success, personal achievement, and fulfillment.

As defined in this booklet, wealth should not coincide with money, but the state of being.

This booklet will show you how to think differently so that you can master whatever you wish.

We have created detailed and easy-to-read chapters on how to transform thoughts, decisions, and choices so that you can gain absolute freedom in areas that negatively impact you.

Having a well-focused mind is needed in every new dimension of your life in order to obtain high achiever success.

I have put years of research into creating this booklet and can ensure it will answer all of your questions regarding creating wealth. Highly impactful people, including multi-millionaires and billionaires, have mentored me. I've studied them and have a good understanding of how successful people operate.

I have taken on and overcome several challenges in my life. It is now my duty to share the knowledge that the top 1%'er master.

The journey wasn't always easy for me. Over the course of my life, I have had to make drastic changes in order to find success.

Every challenge or failure taught me a lesson. Together, these lessons have helped me transition from being submerged in debt and depression to producing positive cash flow and enormous amounts of happiness.

I went from depression to happiness by following the methods highlighted in this booklet.

I was lucky to have been surrounded by mentors and advisors and never had to worry about my financial situation. Life seamlessly made the decision for me.

I am now the owner of two businesses; a real estate company and a financial management agency.

Seeing how some people struggle to make things right, I decided to offer an easy solution in the form of this guide.

This guide highlights both my successes and failures. If you follow the methods prescribed in this booklet, you too could experience exponential wealth as you walk in your destiny.

Chapter 1

Step 1: Creation of a Mind

It can't be overstated; the mind performs one of the most vital functions in the body. Your brain serves for thought and execution. It can act as both a defensive and offensive mechanism and lend itself to individuals choosing good over bad.

You may wonder why I'm directing attention to the brain. In my estimate, the brain is the control center for all things. Therefore, to achieve levels of excellence and to escape persecution, you must assume a mindset that will allow for excellent decision-making. The more right decisions you make, the more wealth you will obtain.

However, before we move ahead, it's important to understand what wealth truly is. I don't define wealth as money but as a state of being.

Who you become will determine if you will be able to achieve wealth. Wealth is an abundance of good and the accumulation of it will make life valuable for all.

When I moved from Virginia to Atlanta in 2008, I didn't see myself as a good person. I was making all wrong decisions. I drove with a suspended license, my car registration was constantly suspended, and I was incarcerated a few times for it.

I hung out and spent money on things that offered zero return.

Fortunately, I had a colleague who saw my potential and began mentoring me. Having good company around me was an attribute of wealth and surrounding myself with positive people helped me distance myself from negativity.

Things didn't always go right for me but it turned out a blessing in disguise. I had an epiphany. I immediately knew that I was born for greater things.

I wanted more out of life and I knew I had to change many things before I could advance in accomplishments.

I thought, If God created everything and God is good, then in order for me to obtain God's blessings and promises, I had to live the way he intended for me to live.

It was at this point that I realized the real reason I was on this planet. God birthed a "new me" through the altering of how I thought.

I found it very important to be around people who were intelligent, had a spiritual connection with God, and very successful in the areas I valued the most.

You must ask yourself, how wealthy are your friends?

Balance is key, and assessing is mandatory. Therefore, build relationships with people who will help you accomplish your goals and not tear them down. Toxic relationships will hold you back from everything you want to accomplish.

In order to change things, I had to begin to think and act differently.

I was purposed to be a leader and a millionaire, and in order to be who God needed me to be; I had to get the mindset of a leader and millionaire.

Perspective is everything. Every aspect of your life must be evaluated for opportunities of growth.

Unfortunately, things aren't bright for the average American according to a CNBC article that said: "more than 76% of Americans live paycheck to paycheck." This analysis further supports that dreams may die because people focus more on survival versus dream building.

While working a 9-5 is not bad, you must understand that every situation, whether good or bad, presents an opportunity for growth.

Not everyone likes the idea of an office job. While office jobs can be exhausting, you can still take time out to pursue what you truly want.

By dedicating at least 30 minutes to your dreams everyday while continuing to do your job will serve for great progress.

Anything you want in life, you must have a mindset that mirror where you want to go. Here's an exercise you can use to help accomplish your goals:

- Challenge the validity of the information you learn.

- Ask yourself, what is my purpose and does my daily routine match where I want to go.

- Commit time and money to accomplishing your dreams. When you commit time and money, you will be pulled toward your dreams.

- Set massive targets that will force you to show up to work everyday.

For instance, if your goal is to become a millionaire in Real Estate in three years, you must know which type of real estate will garner this return in that amount of time, how much time and commitment are you dedicating to this project, and how are you going to track your targeted results. Your goals, results and next steps should be written out each day to hold yourself accountable.

The more you focus on why you were created, the greater the opportunity to clearly understand your destiny.

Most people get influenced by society and do what the world wants them to do instead of listening to their heart or their creator.

Anything you want in life you must have a

mindset that mirror where you want to go

Chapter 2

Step 2: Master Plan

The sure shot way to achieve excellence is by making a decision to commit.

In order to commit to anything, you must sacrifice time and money.

Think about what overarching achievements you want to obtain before you commit to something and once you make a commitment, go all out on one goal. Once you successfully achieve one goal, then begin working on your next goal that is symbiotic to goal number one. Remember that you might not get success right away and you might even have to face challenges such as loneliness and fear of failure but don't let these things affect you. Your commitment will stretch you forward.

According to Cigna, 3 out of 5 people are lonely. Loneliness is found in those who have mental health issues related to anxiety and depression. In my research I found that anxiety and depression is commonly related to the lack of fulfillment. Don't look at loneliness as a bad thing. Loneliness forces you in isolation but anxiety and depression are caused by not being fulfilled. My goal is to show you how being lonely can be good for fulfillment. Isolation will keep you focused and discipline without any toxic interference. When you are achieving what fulfills you, your depression and anxiety will disappear.

To illustrate my point, think about how you feel when you accomplish something that you worked hard for. How do you feel in that moment?

What excitement do you have?

How relaxed do you become?

It can take time but you will learn to appreciate your own company as you progress in life. The good thing about progress is that you learn, which helps you get better.

Learning has been the hallmark of all of my success. Fortunately, I started learning at a very young age. My father owned many businesses. I remember when I was a child I would observe my father working. I observed how he talked, how he conducted his business, and most importantly how people respected him.

Learning helped me grab new skills but not everything I learnt was good. The problem with noticing others is that you end up noticing bad things as well.

As a learner, you must be sure of what you want to learn. Remember what we discussed earlier in this booklet – the value of making the right decisions in all areas of your life.

Choosing to learn something new everyday will lend you great results, however you must make sure that the information you learn is factual and helpful.

Incorrect or misleading information can turn out to be very costly, yet so many of us are caught in the web of wrong data.

People go to school and learn unnecessary information and live their life by it without validating the information that was taught to them. You see this also with parents. Parents raise a child the way they 'want' them to live, and the poor child usually becomes just that rather than raising a child on factual proven methods that garner the highest return on their purpose.

The art of learning is simple, yet highly misunderstood.

In the world we live in, you may never learn something that hasn't already been learnt. Your job is to find the information, validate it, and incorporate it in your life as quickly as possible. The more you learn, the faster and the more you will earn.

Make a list of things that excite you and get you hooked. In simple words, you sort through the thing(s) that drives you or solves a problem. The sorting phase is the revelation phase. Once you determine what you want to do, you must ask yourself, "is this who God created me to be?" People are usually motivated by what they see rather than what they cannot see. 2 Corinthians 5:7 say, "for we walk by faith, not be sight. The problem, however, is that you cannot see the future because you're walking by sight, not by faith.

Think about where you want to be tomorrow and identify people who can positively and willingly help you achieve your goals.

Share your vision and ask them to partner with you.

Open yourself to constructive dissent.

Create thick skin.

Be clear about your vision so that they can best advocate your goal.

Positioning yourself to win begins with having a positive mind in the midst of criticism.

I'd like to quote my former mentor John Maxwell here: "Environment is your incubator and what you allow to occupy your space will either grow

you or diminish you".

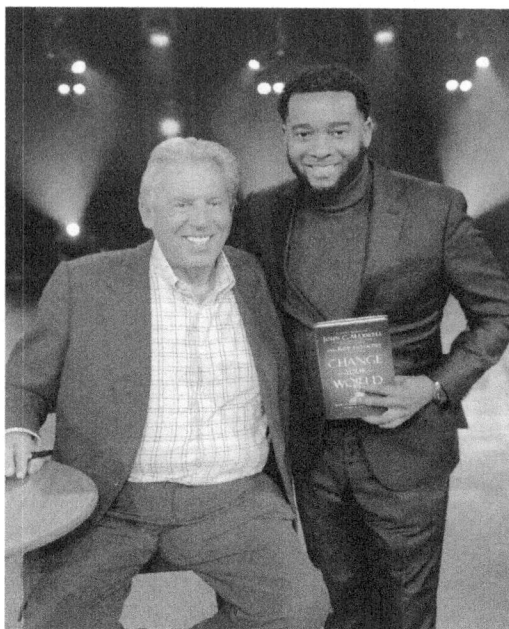

John played a very important role in my life and

helped me understand the value of a healthy

environment and the need to focus on being a good person.

In the planning phase, your emotions are everything. What you see, taste, touch or hear is what usually creates the emotions you feel inside.

Though people confuse movement with achievement, it's actually your emotions that allow you to experience achievement.

Tony Robbins says this best, "Growing and giving should be the pillars of fulfillment."

If you're growing you will feel alive and if you are growing and giving, you will feel super alive.

People have different values and it weighs on their feelings in different ways. The goal here is to learn how to alter your emotional state when things aren't going well.

Your view of the world can help you overcome this negative state. Take a break and revisit your targets. Think about what you wish to achieve.

My targets, for example, are certainty, significance, love, growth and contribution.

Once you identify these targets, determine which targets are most important and begin to incorporate those traits in your life.

If you are growing you will feel alive and if you're growing and giving, you will feel super alive

Chapter 3

Step 3: The Set Up

I like to call this chapter The Set Up because in order to build wealth, your mindset, your master plan and the actions you take must work in tandem.

When I was younger I often had ideas but I failed to have a plan on how I would execute them.

As mentors trained me, I learned that I could not have an idea, without the commitment of taking actions and more importantly the mindset to overcome the challenges of failure and opposition.

I learned very quickly that having an idea alone was not enough.

To be wealthy, you must play the game of the wealthy.

Wealthy individuals are modest, committed, intentional, and understand the power of living conservatively while taking massive action. When you live by these traits, you are able to allocate more resources into your ideas.

There are many wealthy individuals who live conservatively because they understand that in order to achieve wealth you must be calculated in your approach.

Let's consider the Pope. When he traveled across the world a few years ago, he drove a Fiat 500. Yet, he lives in a castle.

You must be willing to sacrifice the luxuries today for the luxuries tomorrow.

This is what you should do once you become committed:

Get Good Credit:

Credit will be the lever to wealth attainment. According to Barron's, the top wealthy earners hold nearly 40% of all debt mortgages in America. When mortgages are obtained, interest tax deductions are received; equity is built, which creates wealth by default. When the wealthy borrow, they do so to fund tax-advantaged, appreciating assets.

Poorer households, on the other hand, rely on debt to pay for post-high school education, transportation, while carrying credit card balances.

Unlike housing, cars and credit cards aren't appreciating assets. In order to receive assets, you must have good credit. The higher your credit, the less interest you have to pay and the lower the monthly payment. Credit should be used to buy income-producing assets. If it doesn't produce income, credit should not be used. Credit allows you to leverage other people's money that creates cash-flow for yourself.

Create a Hybrid-Float:

According to Investopedia, most billionaires are entrepreneurs. When you become an entrepreneur, you have the ability to scale and align your targets for where you want to go. A float will help fund your main goal.

A float is a hidden gem that successful businesses use to raise money before the need to pay it back out. An example of a float would be the process insurance companies use. An insurance company receives premiums and the time from which the premium is paid until the time to pay a claim is considered a float. During this lag in having to pay the claim, the money is invested in producing other assets.

To produce a hybrid float think about what product or service you can offer that will allow you to generate income without the need to exchange time for money. For instance, if your goal is to run a successful global salon brand, create a program/training that customers can purchase and use the funding from it to invest in your main goal of producing a global salon brand.

To be wealthy, you must play the game of the

wealthy

Chapter 4

Step 4: Go Broke

I embraced the idea of being viewed as cheap and consider myself broke even though I still had money in the bank.

Being broke for me means not having money readily available to spend on things that provide me no return. When you spend money, you want it to provide a return in some way.

Pay attention to some of the greatest entrepreneurs, Steve Jobs, Mark Zuckerberg and Jeff Bezos, you'll find that they all started working out of a dorm, basement or house.

Let's consider their start as humble beginnings. Here is a word of advice, never despise small beginnings.

When you first start your business or investing career, you must be frugal as much as possible because according to Warren Buffet, the number 1, and 2 rule in investing is to never lose money.

Sometime ago I created a separate bank account, which I call my *Holy Grail account*. I put away money in this account so that I couldn't touch it. This money was funds I knew I was going to use to get me my first million dollars. The money was from my float, as mentioned previously. I was disciplined, and I knew that if I couldn't touch this money, it would be in safekeeping.

Create a bank account separate from your primary bank account so that you wouldn't be tempted to withdraw.

Every time you get paid, you should have 40% of your money flow into this account.

Whenever I'm looking to invest in a business and birth a new endeavor, I look to my *Holy Grail account* to fund the deal.

Store as much money as you can and when you want to invest, only use a portion of it. Never put all your savings in one investment.

Preparation is one of the critical components of changing your mindset and your financial state.

Work on recalibrating your thoughts and be clear about what you wish to do. Real estate, for example, can be a good investment but you can't just go out and purchase a house. You have to do it in a systematic manner.

Below is my investing process that has worked for me countless times and may help to serve you. This process will require you to be disciplined, but the good news is that it's manageable for anyone to do.

Step 1: Commit.

- Sacrifice time and money to the endeavor.

Step 2: Have a financial goal. Envision your freedom!

- If you don't know where you're going, you'll never reach your destination.

Step 3: Eliminate consumption. If you don't need it, you don't have to have it!

- Decrease your bills by eliminating unnecessary spending.

- Eliminate anything that's not a necessity.

Step 4: Create a float. The float as previously discussed will fund your endeavor.

Step 5: Go broke. Being broke is good!

- If you can't write off the purchase, don't buy it.

Step 6: 40% Rule

- Save 40% of your gross income.
  Determine how much money you have to
  make in order to save 40% of your gross
  income.

Step 7: Invest in real assets. Create recurring
income!

- Real assets are physical assets, for
  example real estate.

- When you invest in real assets you gain
  appreciation in value, which increases your
  return and wealth potential.

- Ensure your passive income exceeds your
  primary income. Passive income is

earnings derived from a rental property, limited partnership or other enterprise in which a person is not actively involved. Passive income is income that produces income without the need of doing physical activity to produce it on a consistent basis. You want your passive income to outweigh your primary day job income.

Step 8: Increase your income.

- Do not quit your day job. Get promoted; ask for a raise or commission plan. I created a promotion playbook for individuals who work in corporate America but want to find ways to get promoted. You can get it by emailing me at service@themichaellindell.com.

- Your goal is to max out the amount of money you can generate.

Step 9: REPEAT.

- The more you repeat this process, the more money you will accumulate!

The richest people in the world either invest or own a business. You must decide, if you want to become wealthy, invest or become a business owner.

Preparation is one of the critical components of

changing your mindset and your financial state

Chapter 5

Step 5: Fear is the Devil

Let's tackle this word we call fear.

One thing I've learned about fear is that fear only appears when we are unsure of the future.

Many people think it is not possible to be a millionaire, especially if they don't already have a lot of money. If you have such a mindset, then it's time to change it because you can never achieve what you do not believe in.

Change your mindset into thinking like a millionaire so that fear doesn't have a place to hide.

So many people put negative emphasis on being a millionaire, but they fail to mention the benefits of having money.

We were always taught to save money and to hold it for a rainy day, but in retrospect, that saying has done more harm than good.

Never save to save but save to invest.

Don't allow the fear of "what if" keep you back from stepping into your next dimension.

In the beginning it may seem tough, but if you follow my plan, you will reach your full potential, and be a millionaire.

If you only saved what you've earned, you'll only have enough money for your life and not enough for your children and for your children's children.

The Bible states that a wise man leaves an inheritance for his children's children. You must provide a nest. Think BIG!

To alleviate fear, you need a good support system such as friends and family. They can push you and help you through this journey.

I have been through this situation and I can assure you that a support system is very important.

When I moved to Atlanta, I was afraid that I was making the wrong decision, until I got to the state and discovered it was the best thing that has happened to me. My business never took off until I moved to Atlanta. Today, I am glad that I made this decision. I was brave, and if you want to succeed, you must be brave as well.

Sometimes a decision can be frightening, but don't allow the fear of what hasn't happened rob you of your joy and financial peace.

The higher you climb, the longer it'll take for you to come down.

Remember scale is your friend. Scale high so that you can encounter hits and remain on top.

I'll share an anecdote, a friend of mine is a pilot and he told me that he had a rough flight when flying to California from New York City. He said the turbulence was bad, and he almost had to perform an emergency landing. Before the emergency landing, he thought of an idea to eliminate the turbulence. He said they typically fly at 35,000 feet, but to stop the turbulence, he had to climb to 45,000 feet. That conversation has always stuck with me. If you encounter problems in any area of your life, rise above it and always remain positive because the universe must honor good.

How can one be afraid of something that hasn't

happened yet

Chapter 6

Step 6: Multiple Streams of Income

Most millionaires will tell you that having multiple streams of income will be essential to building wealth and achieving multi-millionaire status. This is the ultimate truth.

Having multiple streams of income will keep money coming in consistently.

One of the reasons I have been able to achieve my dream is because I have multiple sources of income – 6 to be exact.

Having one stream of income is vulnerable to a shift in the economy. If one stream suffers, the other streams will continue cash flowing. Remember *scale* is your friend.

To have massive amounts of wealth, you must be obsessed with achieving it.

If you want to climb Mount Everest, you must train hard.

If you want big money, you must think big and compound everything good that you do.

I follow this rule as much as I can and pay special attention to the multiplier effect. Whatever I buy must increase my finances, health or happiness. Take a look at your spending and see where you spend most of your money. If where you spend most of your money doesn't provide fulfillment or happiness then you should consider altering where you spend your money.

Even the market suggests you to do the same. A well-known 2010 study by Princeton researchers Daniel Kahneman and Angus Deaton found that people tend to feel happier the more money they make. People's well-being and how they felt about life change once they started making more money. While money alone will not create happiness, the increase of money can certainly make you feel better.

While you need money to make money, cash alone can never be enough if you don't have the right knowledge.

Until you start learning how to invest your money, you won't be able to master the art of increasing your wealth.

Your problem isn't necessarily debt; the problem is that you need to earn more money. Focusing on clearing your debt is the time that is taken away from earning more money.

Earn money, store it, invest it, and repeat it =

multiplier effect.

Not just individuals, but businesses also follow this rule. Look at Apple, they have over 27 products on their website at the time of writing this booklet. This means that Apple has at least 27 streams of income and the company is worth

$2 trillion. Not just Apple, other big names like Wal-Mart and Amazon also reinvest back into their business, not save or spend their revenue on things that won't grow their business.

If you look at any convenient store, they have hundreds of products for sale, i.e.: hundreds of streams of income. Imagine what Wal-Mart streams of income look like. Having multiple streams of income is a hedge that is built to safeguard other assets against any loss in one sector. Compound, compound, compound!

Having money gives you confidence to do more. Compound your savings, compound your mindset, and compound your return on investment.

Look at things from a bigger scale.

There's over $90 trillion dollars on planet earth. That's $90,000,000,000! That means having $1 million of $90 trillion is 0.00000111111%.

Becoming a millionaire is obviously achievable, especially if you live in the richest country on earth. According to Forbes (2020), there are over 18.3 million millionaires in the U.S. There were over 675,000 new millionaires added last year. You must question, "Why weren't you in consideration for this list?"

When obtaining multiple streams of income, you must understand that your first stream is always your day job income. The cash flow that you receive from your day job is how you'll start your investment portfolio. Save as much as you can and place it in your *Holy Grail account*, and then find another income source that is symbiotic to your first flow, and so on.

Real estate / multifamily is a good investment when searching for high returns. Stocks are good investment vehicles if invested passively in a good stock pick such as the S&P 500 or growth stocks.

However, before you decide where to invest, you must plan.

Open multiple bank accounts. Many people have only one bank account and I always ask, how can anyone prioritize their finances with one account?

Can you imagine if Warren Buffet had only one bank account?

Having multiple bank accounts will help you prepare for the next move. Strive to have at least 5 accounts. People with businesses should have at least 12 accounts including their personal 5 accounts.

For individuals, your accounts should include, expense, emergency fund, income, investment aka *Holy Grail*, and entertainment. Entertainment should always be your least funded account.

Here is how your percentage of transfers should look.

- Transfer your day job salary to your income account and from here transfer percentages to other accounts.

- Whatever your total expenses are for the month, you want to divide that amount by how often you get paid and transfer that amount into your expense account every pay. For instance, if your expenses are

$500 a month and you get paid $1,000 weekly, you want to divide $500 by 4 (4 weeks in a month), which will be $125. You want to take $125 each pay period and place it in your expense account and pay your expenses from this account. Your expenses should not be more than 40% of your income. If it's more than 40%, you cannot afford additional expenses.

- 10% of the remaining amount should flow into your emergency account.

- 10% should flow into your entertainment / charity account.

- 40% flow into your investment account.

Remember scale is your friend

Chapter 7

Step 7: Invest In yourself

I'm appalled by how often people choose to invest in things that depreciates.

Investing in yourself will be your greatest investment and should be done first. I learned early on in my life that change was needed for me to be successful. I started investing in myself by researching things that were going to increase my wealth.

I paid for courses that showed me tactics on how to be a better investor and business leader.

I wanted to sit in rooms with people who were smarter than me just to learn and understand business.

I knew what I wanted, and I created a plan to get there. I lost a lot of good friends because I couldn't dedicate my time to hanging out. I wanted more, I wanted to be more, and I wanted to earn more.

You need to be hungry if you want to succeed.

What have you done this month that has helped you invest in yourself?

How much money have you saved to invest in your future?

Who have you purposely met to help you achieve your goals?

How many mentors do you have?

If you can't answer these questions, then it's time for a change.

When you are climbing, you cannot lose sight of what's important.

Before you spend any money, you should ask yourself, is this something that will increase my wealth, health or investment opportunities?

Think about your routine and where you spend your time.

The average person, for example, spends between 1-2 hours a day on social media and it has increased every year since 2012. You have social media activeness increasing while according to CareerBuilder 78% of Americans live paycheck to paycheck. If you also find yourself addicted to social media and realize it isn't adding value to your life then think about changing things.

Unfortunately, most Americans do not understand the power of investing in themselves because most people want things to come to them easily. I'm here to tell you, if you want it easy you will forever live on the government system and in a cycle of depression. Your finances will continue to get smaller while millionaires will continue to increase, and sooner than later the U.S will be too expensive for you to live on your income.

You must earn more if you want to be able to live comfortably. Remember that the market doesn't always remain the same. Every 10 years or so, the United States of America faces some sort of recession. You have business cycle periods: an expansionary period, a peak, a recessionary period, and trough.

If the U.S is in a recessionary period or trough, chances are that people will be laid off.

If the U.S is in a peak or expansionary period, things will end up being too expensive. That's why having multiple streams of income and making more money is important.

As mentioned earlier, saving money doesn't create wealth. The average rate of return in a bank savings account is a measly 0.06%. You cannot save to save because your money will not grow, especially when you take into account inflation.

By you investing in yourself, you automatically

invest in your family

Chapter 8

Step 8: Ways to Become a Millionaire

In this chapter, I want to draw out things you must do to obtain a million dollars. Everything I lay out will require hard work, dedication, tempo and, most importantly, consistency.

I have started 6 companies in the last 10 years and I didn't have a lot of money when I did so. I had to find ways to start these businesses with little money.

My goal at the time was simple – to work a high paying job and fund each of my business ventures. I was successful at doing so, hence I started to incorporate this strategy into each venture.

Most people don't have enough savings as a large number of Americans live from paycheck to paycheck.

You want to keep a steady cash flow and the only way to obtain this is by having a job, which pays you enough to cover your personal expenses and to fund your business.

I am talking about OPM (Other People Money) and using their money to fund your business, which is fine but being able to start successful businesses without debt is much better.

Starting a business with no money isn't realistic since you must pay to register the business, market the business, etc. However, starting a business with little money is possible.

You must decide if you will own a business or become an investor. Owning a business or investing will be the only realistic options in becoming a millionaire.

You must ensure your idea has potential, you're solving a need, and people are interested in what you offer. You must present yourself as an expert in your field. Look at any big name; they appear authentic, which helps people have faith in them.

I realized this early in my life and started to think like a leader. I knew that I needed to think differently.

My surroundings didn't mirror what I wanted. I was around drug addicts, alcoholics, and people who made bad decisions.

I prayed to God to remove people who weren't supposed to be in my life and to change my mindset. The next day my desires of wanting to hang around that crowd changed.

If you want to be successful in business and your career you must be willing to sacrifice something and pay the price for success.

Be around positive people and think about what you need to do to make your venture a success.

The most important factor in building wealth is sales. The more you sell, the more money you'll make. You must be persuasive and able to negotiate a deal when needed. If you are in corporate America and you simply want to get promoted, you must show your managers why you're the best fit for the position. Sales is key if you want to make more money.

As a child I always wanted to buy fake money, but I could never seem to get any because my parents would never buy it. I felt as though if I had fake money, it would activate some sort of return into real money, silly me.

All my friends in middle school had fake money and they would walk around with money bulging out of their pockets.

We would count our money in the back of class and see who had the most. I never had the most money, but I did save my money while the other kids ended up losing theirs. I didn't have real money to buy more fake money, so I saved and eventually I had more money than everyone else.

I shared this story to highlight an important point – to keep track of your finances, no matter how small they are.

I use Personal Capital to manage my money and investments. You need to be able to see what you're spending and how your debt compares to your income on a daily basis.

Your expenses should not be your main concern; instead, spend 95% of your time on income. The issue is usually not your expenses; the problem is that you're not making enough money to hold down your expenses. Below I've highlighted ways to get to a million dollars:

- Sell a $200 product to 5,000 people

- Sell a $500 product to 2,000 people

- Sell a $1,00 product to 1,000 people

- Sell a $2,000 to 500 people

- Sell a $4,000 product to 250 people

- 500 people pay $17/month, for 12 months

- 2,000 people pay $42/month, for 12 months

- 1,000 people pay $83/month, for 12 months

- 500 people pay $167/month, for 12 months

- 250 people pay $333/month, for 12 months

Your expenses should not be your main concern; instead, spend 95% of your time on your income

Chapter 9

Step 9: Controlling Life's Circumstances

Life was never intended to be perfect. It's full of hardships, some worse than others.

I understand how situations can affect one's ability to be successful in their life. I want to help you with this because I have encountered tough times as well.

When I was in the 2nd grade, I was a quiet child. My teacher at the time didn't think I was as mature and talkative as the other students in the class so she recommended that I repeat the 2nd grade.

In retrospect, I couldn't answer why I was so quiet, but one thing I could recall was how I did not like my teacher. It wasn't the fact that I was dumb; I was very observant, and I wanted to learn from my surroundings.

Being held back scarred me. I was ashamed of being a quiet and shy person and did not know how to deal with friends making fun of me. Being scarred at an early age can significantly impact a child's life.

Many people aren't aware of what kids go through until it's too late to fix it. This was a bad time for me, my grades dropped, and I started isolating myself.

The only thing I knew to do to defeat this issue was to create new friends, which overtime proved this wasn't the best decision.

You must be knowledgeable enough to know what's good and what's bad so that you can adapt and change the direction before it's too late.

Remember that you will have to decide between two or more things every now and then. If you are in a problem then look at it from a critical point and understand what's causing the issue.

Determining what you're suffering from will help you start the process of recovery. For example, when you feel pain, you go to a doctor for a diagnosis, so he/she can treat your illness.

A strategy for recovery followed by patience will be your saving grace.

I've been through many difficult situations in my life, but I knew if I identified the problem and its cause, I could overturn the effects of it by working on a solution to overturn it.

Simply put, whatever life throws at you, you have the power to change the narrative if you are willing to assess and do the necessary things to keep moving.

Remember that life throws different challenges including negative people with the sole purpose to distract you from achieving greatness.

When people see you doing well, some may speak against you because they do not understand your purpose.

Do not be discouraged. Your purpose is not designed for others to understand, it is designed for you.

Be aware of your surroundings so that you can eliminate the threat beforehand.

Measure what you can achieve by your potential, not by what has happened to you. Do not let haters deter you. Instead, consider the presence of haters as an affirmation that you are on your way to an extraordinary outcome.

Let me share a small story from the time I got laid off. It was a difficult time. I did not know how I'd manage my finances or pay my bills.

I started getting anxious. I became afraid and depressed. I prayed more than 10 times throughout the day, and I did everything I could do to become healthier.

I went to a doctor who asked questions about my life to understand my situation. She determined that my anxiety was due to my financial concerns. She prescribed medication, which I didn't take because I didn't believe in medicating financial problems. However, I knew that things had to change.

The change began with me. I completely changed my diet. I stopped eating all animal products besides fish. I started working out and running. I felt so good after about a week of changing my diet.

My thoughts were different. I was able to retain more information. My energy levels soared.

The purpose of sharing this story is to show how you can use a bad experience and turn it into something positive.

This experience taught me a lot of things including the importance of having a spiritual connection.

I've had countless situations where I became lost and discouraged. The only remedy was my spiritual connection with God.

Once you learn to build a relationship with God, all things will be made whole. God reminds us "little becomes much when we place it in His hands."

Surround yourself with positive people and things. When you have committed to altered your mind many negative things and people will be thrown at you.

Take the high road. Develop tunnel vision and dig deep into thought; block out everything that's intended to alter your mindset.

My goal is to provide you with steps to build your finances so that you can live abundantly and exalt people and worthy causes.

Determining what you're suffering from will

help you start the process of recovery

Chapter 10

Step 10: Do More

The more you do, the more you'll achieve.

Action will get you moving, but strategy will keep you moving in the right direction. Where you want success, doing more of the *right* things will get you there.

In every aspect of my life I try to do the right thing so that I can worry less about the consequences from terrible decisions. Notice I mentioned choosing right over simply doing more. Pursuing *right* will elevate your confidence and provide a smoother track. I operated with a 95/5 Rule, which suggests spending 95% of your time on offense and 5% of your time on defense. The more you focus on offense, the least amount of time you have reacting to something bad, because your offense will flood-out most problems you encounter.

In every business that I have started, I consistently worked to create a daily initiative to help me move closer to my goals. When I found myself becoming too comfortable, I stretched beyond my comfort level.

The purpose was to become uncomfortable once comfort sets in. Meeting short-term goals will help your long-term goals become more achievable.

Smile more, give more, say more, work more and eventually you'll earn more.

More can be optimized in myriad areas of your life.

There are times where I do not like doing certain things. I force myself to understand the importance of doing them, so I can continue to provide generational wealth for my family.

I used to hate public speaking until I learned that I needed to master it to promote my business. I realized I had to conquer my fear of public speaking to move forward.

Remember that there is nothing excellent about *choosing* to be average. Choose against being in the middle class.

The middle class is not the class you want to be in. You must surge above this threshold if you want wealth.

We were all taught improper practices on how to get money, but we were never taught how to achieve wealth. Playing safe is very risky.

This is why you need to know these three things about money:

- How to get it

- How to keep it

- How to multiply it

Prepare yourself for the naysayers and just keep moving.

You must keep in mind that everyone can obtain wealth, but not everyone will do what it takes to achieve wealth.

Keep moving. Fear can hold you back or propel you forward. I chose the latter. Ignite the *fear flame* within yourself.

Remember, the more you do, the more you'll

earn

Chapter 11

Step 11: Close the Deal

By now you should have a clear understanding of what is required to become wealthy.

If you follow the steps I have outlined in this booklet, you will have the tools you need to become very wealthy. You may ask – what to do once I've mastered all the tips? The answer is simple; multiply the steps.

This portion of the journey is the most exciting because you get to see all your hard work manifest.

When you graduate to this level, it's important to make the right investments.

You must love what you invest in. Moreover, you must be fully aware of what you are taking on. I see many people who try the investing path and entertain deals that they don't love.

You want to love the deal you're working on because it builds your confidence and excitement for the project.

If you're going to work with other investors they will be looking for you to love the deal because it lets them know how much work you put into researching the deal to ensure it will be profitable.

I hope that you will take advantage of all the information I've included in this booklet.

I want to thank you for taking the time to read this booklet. I'm positive that once you put these strategies to use, you will find financial peace.

I wrote this booklet in 6 hours. I wanted to share my success and steps so that you can benefit from what I've learned. After all knowledge is power!

I have always wanted to share valuable content for people who need a financial breakthrough. I wrote this booklet in its simplest form so that it will resonate profoundly.

My goal for this booklet is that you read it at least three times so that you can embed these strategies in your mind. After you read the booklet thrice, I want you to pass the booklet on to a friend. The power of gifting is very important to ensuring your community continues to grow mentally and financially.

We live in the greatest country on earth with unlimited possibilities. This alone makes every idea achievable.

Remember success starts and ends with a made-up mind.

Change your mind and your destiny will follow.

The sooner you change your mindset and unlearn all the poor information that was taught to you about how you should manage your finances, the sooner you will be able to fulfill your dream of a life of wealth and active reciprocity.

Change your mind and your destiny will follow

Made in the USA
Monee, IL
10 February 2021